William Pulteney

The Effects to be expected from the East India Bill

Upon the Constitution of Great Britain, if passed into a Law

William Pulteney

The Effects to be expected from the East India Bill
Upon the Constitution of Great Britain, if passed into a Law

ISBN/EAN: 9783337059187

Printed in Europe, USA, Canada, Australia, Japan

Cover: Foto ©ninafisch / pixelio.de

More available books at **www.hansebooks.com**

THE
EFFECTS

TO BE EXPECTED FROM THE

EAST INDIA BILL,

UPON THE

CONSTITUTION

OF

GREAT BRITAIN,

IF PASSED INTO A

L A W.

BY

WILLIAM PULTENEY, Esq.

FOURTH EDITION, CORRECTED.

TO WHICH IS ADDED A

POSTSCRIPT.

L O N D O N:

PRINTED FOR J. STOCKDALE, OPPOSITE
BURLINGTON-HOUSE, PICCADILLY.

MDCCLXXXIV.

[PRICE ONE SHILLING AND SIXPENCE.]

The Subſtance of what is contained in the following Pages, was intended to have been delivered in Parliament, if other Gentlemen, better entitled to be heard, had not been firſt in the Eye of the Speaker, when I ſeveral times offered myſelf for that purpoſe; but I think it a Public Duty, to declare my Opinion on a matter ſo deeply intereſt-ing to the State.

THE

EFFECTS

TO BE EXPECTED FROM THE

EAST INDIA BILL.

ON the Question which has so
much occupied the Attention
of the Public, concerning the East
India Bill, Gentlemen of known integrity and love for their Country,
have taken different sides; and therefore, the Question must either be
doubtful in itself, or the true grounds

A 2 of

of it have not hitherto been clearly explained. This laft I take to be in
fome degree the fact; and as it is
allowed on all hands to be a bufinefs of great magnitude, I have little
doubt that every one who wifhes to
act an honourable part, will willing-
ly liften to any thing which is fairly
offered, with a view to throw light
upon the matter.

The arguments drawn from Vio-
lation of Charters are fuch, as undoubtedly admit of different opi-
nions: One fet of men may fairly,
perhaps, think, that there is a fufficient
degree of Neceffity in this cafe, to
juftify

juſtify ſo ſtrong an interference of
Parliament, both on account of the
State of the Company's Affairs, and
on account of the Miſconduct of the
Company's Servants in India; and alſo,
becauſe the great ſtake which the Nation has in theſe Concerns, demands
a ſtrong and effectual remedy; whilſt
others may as fairly think, that the
Neceſſity is not in this caſe ſufficiently
urgent: That the Company's Affairs are
in no deſperate condition ; that their
temporary diſtreſs has ariſen from the
general calamity of the National
War; that the Miſconduct of their
Servants abroad, has been exag-
gerated, whether from deſign, or
enthu-

enthufiafm, is immaterial: That by no poffible means, can fuch diftant Dominions enjoy a perfect fyftem of Government; and that by proper Parliamentary Regulations, they may enjoy as confiderable a degree of happinefs and profperity, under the Old Syftem a little corrected, as they are likely to enjoy under the New; which will moft probably fend out a great number of new hungry Perfons, with much the fame fort of principles with thofe who have hitherto vifited that unfortunate country; and that at any rate, it has not been the Trading Concerns of the Company, which have produced

malverfations

malverfations in India, but their Power and Authority over the Natives; which it is ridiculous to fay, cannot inftantly be put into other hands, leaving the Trade upon the fame footing as before any Territorial Power was acquired.

Upon thefe points, the moft upright men may certainly differ in opinion; but there is another queftion, of much greater magnitude, upon which I am apt to think they could not differ, if the argument were fully ftated and rightly underftood; I mean, with regard to the Effects of the prefent Bill upon the Conftitution of this Country.

It

It has been said on this head, that the New Arrangement will increase the Influence of the Crown; which has been explained in this manner. That it will increase the Power of the present Ministers, during the four years that this Act is to be in force; and that if the Nomination is afterwards given to the Crown, it will increase in a very enormous degree the Influence of the Crown itself.

It has also been said, that it will diminish the Influence of the Crown; because the present Nomination being made by his Majesty's present Ministers, and the New Directors being irremove-

able

able by the Crown for four years, it will throw such a weight of power into the hands of the present Ministers, independent of the Crown, that they too will be irremoveable by his Majesty; and if the New Parliament, which must be chosen before the four years expire, shall make a similar New Nomination for the same, or a longer term, instead of permitting the Crown to name, the present Ministers will become independent of the Crown for a new period, which may be renewed again and again, without any limitation of time.

In

In this mode of viewing the Queſtion, ſome of the moſt virtuous Patriots may poſſibly entertain very different ſentiments; ſome may wiſh ſucceſs to the Bill, becauſe they may think it will increaſe the Influence of the Crown, which may appear to them to have been lately too much diminiſhed; others may oppoſe the Bill, for that very reaſon, as believing, that it will increaſe that Influence, which they may think has not been too much, or not ſufficiently diminiſhed. Some again may approve the Bill, becauſe it may appear to them to diminiſh the Influence of the Crown, and becauſe it may throw

a con-

a confiderable degree of power, independent of the Crown, into the
hands of a fet of Gentlemen, who,
though at prefent Minifters, they may
think well difpofed to the Country,
and fafe to be trufted. Others, on the
contrary, may diflike the Bill, becaufe
they may think that we ought to fee
fully the confequences of the late de-
minutions of the Influence of the
Crown, before we proceed to diminifh it farther ; and becaufe they
may not think the prefent Minifters
can be fafely trufted with fo great an
Independent Power even for four years,
much lefs for ever: And many people may think the arguments incon-

B 2   fiftent,

fiftent, which contend that the Bill will both increafe and diminifh the Influence of the Crown; and that therefore, neither of the affertions. can be relied on; but that the only point to be attended to is, whether the Bill promifes a better Admini-ftration of our Affairs in India' than formerly; and that as the Bill is only to endure for four years, we may truft that Parliament will not renew it, if any dangerous confe-quences are found to have arifen during that fhort period.

But in order to judge fairly of this Bill, it is fit to ftate clearly
what

what appears to be the intention of thofe who bring it in; and then to confider the Effects which that will produce upon the Conftitution of this Government.

The intention of the Bill is, to veft the whole Powers of the Eaft India Company in *Seven* Directors, whofe names were moved by the prefent Secretary of State, and adopted by the Houfe of Commons. They are to hold their offices for four years, removable, like the Twelve Judges, by an Addrefs of either Houfe of Parliament, and not by any other power : And

for

for managing the Commercial Affairs
of the Company, *Nine* Gentlemen,
moved for and adopted in the fame
manner, are to affift them, fubject to
their controul, and removable by them.

The effect of this is, to veft in thefe
Seven Directors the whole Influence
of the Offices of every kind in India,
and at home, belonging to the Company; and the whole Influence arifing
from the tranfactions of their Trade
here, in the purchafe of goods for
exportation, furnifhing fhipping, ftores,
and recruits ; the Influence arifing
from the method of felling their goods,
by bringing forward or keeping back
goods

goods at the fales, or giving indulgen‑
cies as to payments, fo as to accommo‑
date thofe who are meant to be fa‑
voured; the Influence arifing from
the favour they may fhew to thofe
who are now in England, and have
left debts or effects in India, as to the
mode of bringing home and recover‑
ing their fortunes; the Influence of
contracts of all kinds in India; of pro‑
motions, from ftep to ftep; of favour in
the Inland and Export Trade; of intimi‑
dation with refpect to every perfon now
there, who may come home with a
fortune; both with regard to recover‑
ing his debts, and the means of re‑
mittance, and with regard to enqui‑
ries

ries into his conduct; the Influence
upon foreign Companies, or foreign
States, who have eftablifhments in
that Country,—who, in return, may
have the means of acting upon In-
dividuals in this Country; the Influence upon the native Princes of India, fome of whom have already
found the way of procuring the Elec-
tions of Members of Parliament; and
many other means of Influence, which
it is impoffible to forefee, or to
trace.

The amount of the whole cannot
be computed. It has been called
equal

equal to two or three millions a year, for the fum paid in cafh to the Civil and Military Officers, is alone faid to amount to more than one million a year; but there can be no doubt that its magnitude is very great and exten- five indeed, and that it may produce very remarkable confequences.

This power is not, indeed, taken from the Crown; but it is placed in new hands, who are independent during four years, equally of the Crown and of the People. Before this Bill, it was placed in twenty-four Directors, cho- fen by the Proprietors at large. The Election was at firft annual; but, by an Act paffed feveral years ago, fix

C   Direc-

Directors were to go out by rotation every year, and fix new Directors to be chosen: So that each Director was elected for four years; after which he was to go out, and could not be re-elected for a certain interval.

By this means, the Patronage of the Company was, in the first place, divided amongst twenty-four, instead of seven; and these twenty-four consisted of very different descriptions of men, with different, and often opposite, connections, not named by one man, or one party, but chosen by the Proprietors of India Stock; to whom alone they felt themselves indebted for their situations.——

It

It was, secondly, employed not to effect an Influence in Government, to which none of that description of men aspired, but was applied to shew gratitude to those who had assisted in their Election, or from whom they might expect a similar support hereafter, and amongst their private friends and connections. Government, no doubt, must have had a share of the favours bestowed by the Directors; but it was not of a very important nature, nor very extensive. It was not a share independent of the Crown, but passed to the Minister of the Day. The Directors, having no joint object of obtaining the power of governing the

State,

State, could never unite in directing the Patronage of the Company to acquire that power; and their favours were diffufed very generally over the kingdom, with little or no regard to the diftinctions of State Parties.

The whole of this Patronage will be diverted into a different channel; and being put into the hands of perfons named by one of the State Parties, it may be fuppofed that it will in future be chiefly employed as a State Engine; and that it muft produce very important and ferious Effects upon the future Government of this Country.

The

The Secretary of State, in the courſe of the progreſs of the Bill in the Houſe of Commons, took occaſion to declare, that he had never ſaid, that at the end of the four years the No-mination of the ſeven Directors would be given to the Crown; but added, that he feared it might. The ob-ject of which declaration might poſ-ſibly be, to quiet, in ſome degree, the fears of thoſe who dreaded an in-creaſe of Influence in the Crown; but the latter part of the declaration, was at the ſame time well adapted to keep up the hopes of thoſe who favoured the Bill, from an honeſt or

an

an interested wish to increase, by this means, the Influence of the Crown.

But men, accustomed to affairs, are apt to look more to the characters and principles of those who speak, than to what they say, in the moment: They are apt to look to the nature of the human mind, in order to judge how men will act on great and important occasions. It is not any part of the principles of the Party to whom the Secretary of State has attached himself, to increase the Influence of the Crown; but they, like men of talents, in all ages, cannot be supposed averse to an inde-

, pendent

pendent power in themfelves, which they may think it impoffible they fhould ever abufe. To that Party, this Country owed, in a great meafure, the Revolution; and the gratitude of the Nation can never overpay them, unlefs by furrendering both King and People into their hands: But the fame Party, when in Power, undoubtedly extended the Influence of the Crown by Corruption, beyond the example of any former period; and they extended that Influence to fuch a degree, that the Crown found itfelf ftrong enough to difpenfe with their fervices. They have again been inftrumental in reducing that Influence

very

very confiderably, and they have been once more placed in Office. Nobody will believe, that it is now their object, by this Bill, to give, after four years, or at any future period, a new Influence to the Crown, which would not only far furpafs what the Crown has lately loft, but more than double what it ever at any time enjoyed; for if they did give it, the weight of that Party in the fcale of Government, would no longer be felt.

No perfon can therefore ferioufly doubt, that it is the intention of the prefent Minifters to renew this Bill in fuch a manner, as to preferve the

full

full power of Indian Patronage in
their own hands; and I have no doubt
that the utmoſt pains will be taken,
during theſe four years, to reconcile
the Nation to the meaſure: I am per-
ſuaded moſt fully, that great exer-
tions will at firſt be made, to reform
all glaring abuſes in India; but when
once the power here is fully fixt, and applied to Political Influence, we may be
ſure, that no complaints will come home
from India to this country againſt Fa-
vourites; for who will dare to make
a complaint? and every circumſtance
in the conduct of this Bill convinces
me, that the preſent plan decidedly
is, to veſt the whole Power and Patronage of India in the Members of

D   the

the prefent Adminiftration, not only
during four years, but as long as India
fhall belong to this kingdom.

If it is faid, that Parliament, at the
end of four years, may interpofe; it is
to be confidered, that an Adminiftration poffeffed of the Power of India,
is not removeable in time of Peace,
either by the Crown or by the voice
of the People; and as a General Election muft come on in four years, and
may come on much fooner, they muft
know very little of the ftate of Elec-
tions in this Ifland, who think that,
with the whole power of Government, and the whole power of India,
fo powerful a Party in this kingdom,

will

will not be able to take their meafures
fo, as to have nothing to fear from a
future Parliament.

The only queftion therefore to be
confidered is, What will be the Effects
of this change in the Conftitution ?
And it is upon this queftion, when
more fully explained, that I think
honourable men cannot poffibly differ,
whatever predilection they may natu-
rally have for particular men, or particular defcriptions of men, or particular parties.

It is poffible, that all perfons may
not have particularly turned their at-

tention,

tention to what it is that conſtitutes
the very eſſence of this Conſtitution:
We all know that it is the very beſt
Conſtitution upon the face of the
globe, becauſe we all feel its benign
influence; we all know that its out-
ward form, conſiſts of King, Lords,
and Commons: But many are not ap-
priſed of the particular cauſe, that our
Government has not been hitherto ſub-
ject to thoſe fatal diſaſters, which have
attended all former ſyſtems, where the
People have enjoyed a great ſhare in
the Government of their Country. I will
ſhortly ſtate my idea of it, but I do not
claim the merit of the diſcovery; I
take it from a moſt ingenious Author,

to

to whom the Republic of Letters, and Mankind in general, are greatly indebted.

In Republican Governments, thofe who were intrufted by the People, were thereby conftantly placed in a fituation which gave them a perfonal intereft, feparate and diftinct from the People at large, which neceffarily excited views and confiderations by no means in unifon with the fecurity and freedom of the general mafs. The confequence always was, that the People were betrayed by every new Favourite, and the power and confequence of a few perfons was fuccef-

fively

sively established, which in time became
so grievous, that the People were pre-
pared for accepting of the despotism
of one person, as preferable to the arbitrary Government of a few of their
fellow citizens. Whereas in our Government, the persons intrusted by the
People to exercise their powers, as
Representatives, have no permanent
separate interest, nor any executive
authority whatsoever; their only
power is to propose and consent to
Laws, and to controul the exercise
of the Executive, which is placed in
the Prince: Their interest and
that of the People is the same;
they cannot betray the People without

out at the fame time betraying themfelves: And, as no individual can obtain the exercife of Executive Powers, except at the will of the Prince, by whom he may be deprived of it at pleafure, it is the intereft of every one, to unite in preventing the power of the Prince from rifing to an improper height; becaufe he may himfelf be the firft to feel the effects of it. Not that particular men may not fometimes be weak enough to fancy themfelves fo perfectly fecure in the favour of the Prince, as to wifh to increafe the power of the Sovereign beyond due limits; but the general feelings of all being very ftrongly directed to withftand the extenfion of

the

the Sovereign Power, the Representatives of the People have in general
been faithful to their truft, with refpect to that effential point, of refift-
ing the encroachments of Power; not
from any fuperior virtue in the inha-
bitants of this ifland, but from the
form of the Conftitution, which gave
the Reprefentatives of the People no
feparate and diftinct interest from the
People at large.

This happy circumftance, peculiar
to our form of Government, arifes from
our having, as a part of it, a King,
in whom is vefted the whole Executive Power, but who has not the power

of

of making Laws, nor the power of controuling Judges and Juries, nor the power of levying Money. He has, however, fufficient power for every good and ufeful purpofe; and the exift-ence of fuch a branch in our Go-vernment, has this important effect, that as no Favourite of the People can, with us, afpire at the Sceptre, nor can ever hold more than a precarious power at the will of the Crown, all who are actuated by ambition, imme-diately perceive the neceffity of main-taining equal laws and of fupporting the general freedom, in which their own fecurity is neceffarily involved. They and the whole People are

E therefore

therefore united to guard againſt the Executive Power, which poſſeſſes alone a permanent pre-eminence, and which, by being equally formidable to all, produces a general motive of intereſt to reſiſt it.

But if the balance were turned the other way, and it were in the power of Popular Leaders to maſter the Crown, that neceſſary branch of the Conſtitution would be annihilated as to every uſeful purpoſe, and the ambition of every man would take a new direction; the Leaders would from that moment come to have a ſeparate perſonal intereſt, diſtinct

from

from that of the People; equal laws would be no longer an object to them, but only laws which might favour their individual power and preeminence. The Liberty of the Prefs, fo effential to General Liberty, would foon be at an end; for it does not exift in any State, where the power is in the hands of a few, any more than it exifts in abfolute Governments: It exifts not in Holland, nor in Venice; nor did it exift at Rome. We would experience, in a fhort time, all the mifchiefs of an Ariftocratical form of Government, and would probably at laft be driven, like the people of Sweden,

to

to feek a miferable relief by throwing ourfelves into the arms of an abfolute Prince.

Moft of the Governments in Europe were formerly limited Monarchies; but many of them have been deftroyed by meafures of this very fort, by putting into other hands part of the Executive Power of the State, with a view to controul more completely the power of the Prince; and the People have at laft been willing to render the King abfolute, in order to be relieved of what they thought a more grievous yoke.

I would

I would earneſtly recommend to all who have doubts upon this ſub-ject, that they would peruſe the four following ſhort chapters of Mr. De Lolme's excellent Treatiſe on the Conſtitution of England, viz. Book 2d, Cap. 9th, 10th, 17th, and 19th, of the Engliſh Edition, 1781.

In the 9th chapter the Author ſhews, that in Republican Govern-ments the People are neceſſarily be-trayed by thoſe in whom they truſt; but in the 10th chapter he explains, by what happy mechaniſm in our State we are relieved and ſecured from that fatal diſadvantage; and

that

that with us " the People can give
" their confidence, without giving
" power over themfelves; they can
" appoint Truftees, and yet not give
" themfeives mafters." In the 17th
chapter he points out, by what circum-
ftances in our form of Government,
the Crown has been enabled, without a dependent mercenary army, to
maintain its neceffary authority, al-
though that authority is the object of
jealoufy to every part of the People:
And in the 19th chapter he fets in a
ftrong and clear light, the very great
and fatal danger of transferring any
part of the power which ought to be
vefted in the Crown, to any other
order

order of men in the State; for this
is a very different queſtion from that
of aboliſhing altogether, any power
in the Crown, which may be thought
too great or too dangerous. I cannot help tranſcribing a ſhort para-
graph from this chapter: " If through
" the unforſeen operation of ſome
" new regulation, made to reſtrain
" the Royal Prerogative, or through
" ſome ſudden public revolution, any
" particular bodies, or claſſes of in-
" dividuals, were ever to acquire a
" perſonal independent ſhare in the
" exerciſe of the governing authority,
" we ſhould behold the virtue and
" patrictiſm of the Legiſlators, and
                              " great

" great men, immediately ceafe with
" its caufe, and Ariftocracy, as it
" were watchful of the opportunity,
" burft out at once, and fpread itfelf
" over the kingdom."

Thefe chapters were not wrote
with a view to the prefent Queftion;
but they are applicable to it in fo
direct a manner, that they will al-
moft appear to have been wrote for
the exprefs purpofe. That Author's
doctrines are the refult of a cool, dif-
paffionate inveftigation of the principles of our Government, and therefore are free from all fufpicion of
Party views. They will lead to
very

very deep and ferious reflections in the breaft of every man who values the Liberty he has hitherto enjoyed.

If the arguments which, from the affiftance of this excellent Author, I have ventured to ufe, are of any weight, they preclude all enquiry into the characters of thofe who have brought forward this meafure, or of thofe who are named as Directors in the Bill. Let their characters be what they may, it does not alter the necef-fary effects of fuch a change in the Conftitution. Thefe confequences muft and will neceffarily follow, in what-ever hands fo dangerous a power is

F   placed;

placed; and it is a miserable system of Government, which depends for its good effects upon the personal worth or integrity of those who are intrusted with great power: Sure I am, that those who rely on such security, will be always most miserably disappointed at last.

After what I have said, it is unnecessary to add another objection to the Bill, namely, that we shall involve the personal interest, or rather the personal power, of a formidable Aristocracy in this kingdom, in the preservation of our Indian Territories, at all hazards. This may be attended

tended with the moſt ſerious conſe-
quences, and may expoſe this Country,
not only to certain bankruptcy, but
to the being left, at a critical moment, almoſt defenceleſs, and open
to invaſion.

But it has been objeƈted, that no
other leſs exceptionable Plan for India
has been propoſed, and that ſomething muſt be done.—I am no Advo-
cate for the Bill offered to the Houſe
of laſt year; but certainly the giving
abſolute power to a Governor-General
in India, removeable by the Crown,
did not endanger this Conſtitution,
like the preſent Bill; nor could the

Patronage

Patronage propofed to be given to him of Offices to be held in India, be by that means equally applied, to operate upon this Conftitution. It could not operate at all againft the neceffary power of the Crown; and it could not, fo delegated, and at fuch a diftance, operate very materially in favour of the precarious Minifter of the Day.

The Propofers of this Bill have fhewn their confcioufnefs, that their New Directors cannot govern India, any more than the Old, without a variety of new regulations; for they have brought in a Bill which contains

many

many fuch regulations. Why fhould not the experiment be firft tried un-der thefe new regulations. The Old Directors, when aided by thefe regulations, when reftrained by the controul of Minifters, and of Par-liament, and relieved, as to the ap-pointing and recalling Officers, from the controul of the General Court, may, I truft, be able to govern India, in as perfect a manner as a diftant Dominion fo peculiarly circumftanced is capable of being governed. We ought to try every experiment before rifking the confequences of fo mate-rial a change as this, in our prefent Conftitution; and many thinking men

begin

begin to pronounce, that the total
lofs of India to Britain would be a
misfortune of inferior magnitude, to
the neceffary blow which the prefent
Bill would give to the Liberties of
this Country.

If this Bill fhould pafs, it will be
a call upon every man of every rank,
who is not embarked as an acceffary
to the meafure, to unite in a fyfte-
matic body to bring about its Repeal.
The queftion of General Warrants,
the queftion of the Middlefex Election, and all the Conftitutional Topics
which have agitated mens' minds in
modern times, are as nothing, when

put

put in comparifon with it. The fate of the Kingdom, the freedom of Britons, will ultimately depend upon the effect of their united efforts, to reftore the breach that will thus be made in the beft Conftitution which the admiring World has ever beheld.

POSTSCRIPT.

POSTSCRIPT.

SINCE the firſt Edition was printed, it has occured to me, that I ought to have obſerved, when I ſtated the objection, " that no leſs objec- " tional Plan for India had been pro- " poſed, and that ſomething muſt be " done," that this is not a ſort of anſwer which Miniſters are entitled to make uſe of in Parliament; becauſe it is their buſineſs, as poſſeſſed of Of- ficial Information, to bring forward Plans ; and it is the buſineſs of other Members to make objections. If Miniſters cannot anſwer theſe objec-

tions,

tions, nor introduce Claufes to remove them, it is their bufinefs to profit by the objections, and bring forward a better Plan. Not that any Member ought to refufe to give every affift-ance, and every light in his power; but I hope it will never be a reafon for accepting a bad Plan, becaufe thofe who have not fituations of Re-fponfibility are not ready to produce a better Plan for the Minifter to adopt.

When I fuggefted the idea of tak-ing away from the General Court of Proprietors, the power of ap-pointing and recalling Officers, I did it merely to remove the argu-

G ment

ment ufed by the Secretary of State, for naming in Parliament the *Seven New* Directors; namely, that the prefent Directors, becaufe controuled by the Proprietors, are difabled from all Authority over their Servant abroad; That controul of the Proprietors can only weaken the Authority of the Directors over their Servants abroad, when it interferes as to the naming, recalling, and punifhing Officers; and it is a full anfwer to fay, that Parliament may take away that controul of the Proprietors, and give the Directors full power, as to the naming and recalling; but it does not fol low, that the Election of Directors fhould be alfo taken from the Proprietors.

My

My prefent opinion, however, is, that it would be hazardous to leave no controul in the Proprietors, upon thofe who are appointed by the Directors; and that though it would be right to give the Directors the exclufive power of naming to all Offices (fubject, as to the appointment of Members of the Supreme Council, and of all Governors or Prefidents, to the Negative of the Crown) yet that the Proprietors, as well as the Directors, fhould have the power of recalling every perfon in office abroad, leaving it folely to the Directors to name others; and that both the Proprietors and Directors fhould have

G 2   the

the power of ordering Profecutions,
and of inflicting Punifhments; fo
that the Refolutions of either of thefe
Bodies, as to recalling, profecuting,
and punifhing, fhould be carried
into execution without controul of
the other Body. In fhort, that neither fhould have the power of fcreening Offenders; but that the permanent Body alone, viz. the Directors,
fhould have the Executive Power.
By this means, the Government of
India would in fome degree refemble
the Government of Britain. The
King can name the Officers; but
Parliament can addrefs his Majefty
to remove, and can, as well as
the

the King, order Profecutions for all Offences.

There is little danger in trufting a numerous Affembly with the power of demanding punifhment, becaufe, except in a moment of fudden heat, they are always too mild; but there is great danger in trufting them with the appointment to Offices of Emolument, or with the power of fcreening Delinquency. There is alfo great danger, on the other hand, in leaving the Nominees of the Directors free of all controul, except from thofe who appoint them.

The

The Proprietors, I think, may also be safely trufted with a con-troul, as to all Expenditure of Money; but I fhould not think it fafe to give them the power of making Grants of Money to any individual.

F I N I S.

This Day is publifhed, for J. Stockdale, *oppofite Burlington-Houfe, Piccadilly, in Three Volumes Octavo, Price Fourteen Shillings and Sixpence,*

A FULL and Authentic Account of the feveral DEBATES on Mr. FOX's EAST INDIA BILL, in the HOUSE of COMMONS, on Thurfday the 27th November, and on Monday the 1ft. and Monday the 8th December: And in the HOUSE of LORDS, on Tuefday the 9th, Monday the 15th, Tuefday the 16th, and Wednefday the 17th of December, 1783. Including the feveral Papers containing a true Statement of the Company's Affairs: Lifts of the Divifions; of the Abfentees; and of thofe who retired before the Divifions commenced.

Together with
Authentic Copies of Mr. Fox's Two EAST INDIA BILLS, the Arguments of the Counfel againft one of them, in behalf of the Court of Directors and Court of Proprietors, at the Bar of both Houfes of Parliament.

ALSO,
The DEBATES in the HOUSE of COMMONS from Tuefday, Dec. 18th, to Wednefday December 24th, on the STATE of the NATION; on the various Motions. Refolutions, and Addreffes, during that period; with his Majefty's Anfwers to the Addreffes.

AND LIKEWISE,
The DEBATES in the HOUSE of COMMONS, from Monday the 12th, to Friday the 16th of January, 1784; containing the very interefting Debates on Mr. PITT's EAST INDIA BILL, with a CORRECT COPY of the BILL.
The whole compiled and revifed in the beft manner poffible; forming one of the moft complete and interefting Parliamentary Works ever offered to the Public; and may be had feparate or together.

BEAUTIES

BEAUTIES

OF

FOX, NORTH, AND BURKE.

This Day is publiſhed, Price 3s. 6d.

Embelliſhed with a beautiful Frontiſpiece of thoſe remarkable Characters, taken from the Life by an eminent Artiſt ;

Together with an ADDRESS to the PUBLIC; and a Series of Facts to the Friends of the Coalition ;

And a copious Index to the whole, in the courſe of which, the following charges, amongſt many others, appear to be brought againſt Lord North, by Mr. Fox or Mr. Burke :

LORD NORTH
charged with a want of candour and conſcience 1
accuſed of treachery and falſhood - - 3
charged with negligence and incapacity - ib,
accuſed of raſhneſs - 4
leads the Houſe of Commons blindfold ib.
deſcribed as a blundering pilot - - 5
charged with the loſs of a whole continent ib.
pronounced a Tory, and hence an enemy to freedom - - ib.
charged with breach of promiſe - 7, 32
never twice of the ſame temper or of the ſame opinion - - 7
ſuſpected of being bribed - - ib.

LORD NORTH
his conduct pronounced inſolent and contemptuous - - ib.
accuſed of the deſign of ſpreading arbitrary power throughout the empire - - 9
charged with inſolence and temerity - 10
being credulous - ib.
compared to Sir Robert Walpole for corruption, and ſaid to have loſt half the empire by it - 11
charged with ignorance 21
charged in the moſt direct terms with the loſs of America - -. ib.
accuſed of avarice and ambition - 24
charged with partiality ib.
his views pronounced diſhoneſt and corrupt 27

BEAUTIES of FOX, NORTH, and BURKE.

Printed for J. STOCKDALE, opposite Burlington-
Houfe. Piccadilly.